BUILD-A-LAB!
SCIENCE EXPERIMENTS

Physics Projects
with a
LIGHT BOX

YOU CAN BUILD

ROBERT GARDNER

Enslow Publishers, Inc.
40 Industrial Road
Box 398
Berkeley Heights, NJ 07922
USA

http://www.enslow.com

Library of Congress Cataloging-in-Publication Data

Gardner, Robert, 1929–
    Physics projects with a light box you can build / Robert Gardner.
        p. cm. — (Build a lab! science experiments)
    Summary: "Introduces information on physics through a variety of related experiments using a light box that the reader can build"—Provided by publisher.
    Includes bibliographical references and index.
    ISBN-13: 978-0-7660-2810-4 (alk. paper)
    ISBN-10: 0-7660-2810-0 (alk. paper)
    1. Physics—Experiments—Juvenile literature. 2. Science projects—Juvenile literature. I. Title.
    QC33.G37 2008
    530.078—dc22
                                                        2006100566

Printed in the United States of America

10 9 8 7 6 5 4 3 2 1

To Our Readers: We have done our best to make sure all Internet Addresses in this book were active and appropriate when we went to press. However, the author and the publisher have no control over and assume no liability for the material available on those Internet sites or on other Web sites they may link to. Any comments or suggestions can be sent by e-mail to comments@enslow.com or to the address on the back cover.

Photo Credits: Enslow Publishers, Inc.

Illustration Credits: Jonathan Moreno

Cover Illustrations: Enslow Publishers, Inc.; Jonathan Moreno (background); Shutterstock (bulb).

CONTENTS

EXPERIMENTS WITH A ✿ SYMBOL FEATURE IDEAS FOR YOUR SCIENCE FAIR.

CONTENTS

EXPERIMENTS WITH A ❧ SYMBOL FEATURE IDEAS FOR YOUR SCIENCE FAIR.

INTRODUCTION

L ight is the earth's only external source of energy. It is vital to life. Without it, plants would be unable to make food. Without plants, which are at the base of the food chain, animals could not live.

It was Sir Isaac Newton (1643–1727) who first developed a satisfactory theory about light. It was Newton, too, who showed that sunlight could be separated into all the colors of the rainbow and then put back together to reform white light. Newton believed that light was made up of tiny, fast-moving particles. Later, other scientists carried out experiments that indicated that light was like waves. Today, we consider light as having properties of both waves and particles. Regardless of their true nature, the properties of light will become evident as you do the experiments in this book.

To investigate light, you will first build a light box. The light box and the materials that go with it will allow you to do experiments that will help you to understand light. The experiments involve reflection, refraction (the bending of light), and colored light, which lends so much beauty to the world. One nice thing about doing light experiments is that you can literally see the results.

If you find that you enjoy experimenting to learn about light, you may want to study physics in high school and college. Learning about light might even become part of your life's work if you choose an occupation such as physicist, optician, optometrist, ophthalmologist, or optical technician.

At times, as you carry out the activities in this book, you may need a partner to help you. It would be best if you work with someone who enjoys experimenting with light as much as you do. In that way, you will both enjoy what you are doing. **This book will alert you to any danger involved in doing an experiment. In some cases, to avoid danger, you will be asked to work with an adult. Please do so.** We don't want you to take any chances that could lead to an injury.

Like any good scientist, you should record your ideas, sketches, notes, calculations, questions, and anything you can conclude from your investigations in a notebook. By so doing, you can keep track of the information you gather and the conclusions you reach. Keeping a good notebook will allow you to refer to things you have done and help you in doing other projects in the future.

SCIENCE FAIRS

Some of the investigations in this book contain ideas you might use for a science fair project. Those experiments are indicated with a 🏅 symbol. However, judges at science fairs do not reward projects or experiments that are simply copied from a book. For example, a diagram of the electromagnetic spectrum would not impress most judges; however, finding unique ways to measure the wavelength of light from infrared to ultraviolet would certainly attract their attention.

Science fair judges tend to reward creative thought and imagination. It is difficult to be creative or imaginative unless you are really interested in your project; therefore, try to choose an investigation that appeals to you. Before you jump into a project, consider, too, your own talents and the cost of the materials you will need.

If you decide to use an experiment or idea found in this book for a science fair, you should find ways to modify or extend it. This should not be difficult because you will discover that new ideas come to mind as you carry out investigations. Ideas will come to you that could make excellent science fair projects, particularly because the ideas are your own and are interesting to you.

If you decide to enter a science fair and have never done so, you should read some of the books listed in the "Further Reading" section. These books deal specifically with science fairs and provide plenty of helpful hints and useful information that will help you avoid the pitfalls that sometimes plague first-time entrants. You'll learn how to prepare appealing reports that include charts and graphs, how to set up and display your work, how to present your project, and how to relate to judges and visitors.

THE SCIENTIFIC METHOD

When you do a science project, especially one with your own original research, you will need to use what is commonly called the scientific method. In many textbooks you will find a section devoted to the subject. It will probably tell you that the scientific method consists of a series of steps. The book may even list the steps in a particular order.

Many scientists will tell you that there is no set pattern that leads him or her to new knowledge. Each investigation is unique and requires different techniques, procedures, and ways of thinking. Perhaps the best description of the scientific method was given by Nobel-prize-winning physicist Percy Bridgman. He said that the scientific method is doing one's best with one's mind.

The idea that there is a single scientific method that all scientists follow probably came about because of the way scientists report their findings. All good scientific projects try to answer a question, such as "Does light travel in a straight line?" Once you have a question, you will need to form a hypothesis. A hypothesis is an idea of what you think will happen. Perhaps you think that light does travel in a straight line. Your experiment should then test your hypothesis.

Scientific reports are very similar in format and include the question, the hypothesis, the experimental procedure, the results, and a conclusion. You will follow a similar format when you prepare the report for your project.

SAFETY FIRST

Most of the projects included in this book are perfectly safe. However, the following safety rules are well worth reading before you start any project.

1. **Never look directly at the sun or any source of bright light! The light can damage your eyes.**

2. Do any experiments or projects, whether from this book or of your own design, under the supervision of a science teacher or other knowledgeable adult.

3. Read all instructions carefully before proceeding with a project. If you have questions, check with your supervisor before going any further.

4. Maintain a serious attitude while conducting experiments. Fooling around is dangerous to you and to others.

5. Wear approved safety goggles when you are working with a flame or doing anything that might cause injury to your eyes.

6. Have a first-aid kit nearby while you are experimenting.

7. Do not put your fingers or any object other than properly designed electrical connectors into electrical outlets.

8. Never let water droplets come in contact with a hot lightbulb.

9. Never experiment with household electricity.

Never leave your light box unattended while the bulb is turned on. When you are done with an experiment, turn off

10. the bulb and unplug the cord from the wall. Let the bulb cool before you touch it.

BUILDING A LIGHT BOX

To build your own light box, gather the items found in the materials list. Let's get started.

1. Place the open end of an empty portable light socket against the middle of one end of the box. Draw a circle around the edge of the socket. **Ask an adult** to use a sharp knife to cut out the circle you drew. Leave the penciled circle so the socket will fit tightly when you push it through the hole. Add a clear 60-watt lightbulb with a straight-line filament to the socket. Turn the bulb so that the straight filament is vertical as shown in Figure 1.

You Will Need

- **AN ADULT** !
- **empty, sturdy, cardboard shoebox that held men's shoes (about 38 cm [15 in] long x 20 cm [8 in] wide x 13 cm [5 in] deep)**
- **sharp knife**
- **portable light socket and cord**
- **pencil**
- **clear 60-watt lightbulb with a straight-line filament**

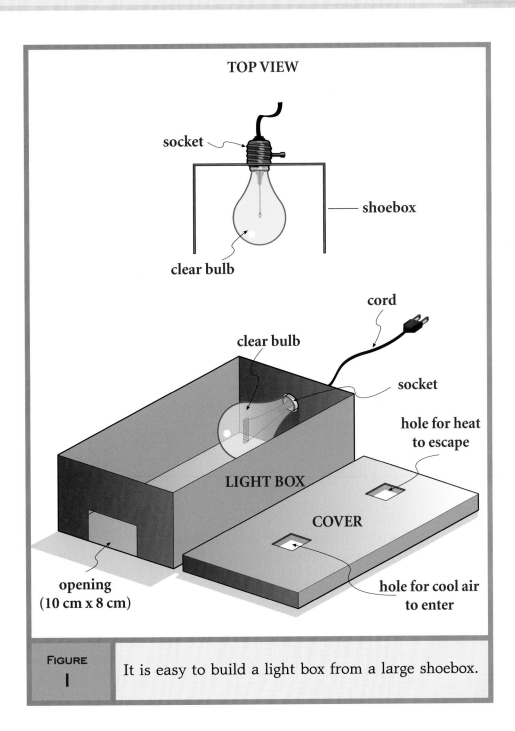

TOP VIEW

socket

shoebox

clear bulb

cord

clear bulb

socket

hole for heat
to escape

LIGHT BOX

COVER

opening
(10 cm x 8 cm)

hole for cool air
to enter

FIGURE 1   It is easy to build a light box from a large shoebox.

2. **Ask the adult** to cut a small hole about 2.5 cm (1 in) square from the box's top at a point above the bulb. This will allow heat from the lightbulb to escape. Also, **ask the adult** to cut another hole in the top to allow cool air to enter as shown in Figure 1.

3. Finally, **ask the adult** to cut a rectangular hole about 10 cm (4 in) wide and 8 cm (3 in) high across the middle bottom of the box at the end opposite the bulb. The box, with its top beside it, should now look like Figure 1.

   Your next task will be to make several different masks that can be placed over the rectangular opening. The masks will cause different light patterns to come out of the box.

MAKING MASKS

All the masks can be built on the same basic wooden frame, which you can make from Popsicle sticks, as shown in Figure 2a. The sticks, which are about 11.3 cm (4.5 in) long, can be obtained from a craft or hobby store.

1. Use only sticks that are very straight to make the frames. You will use 4 sticks to make each of the 9 basic frames, so gather 36 sticks, plus 13 others you will need later. Place a small drop of glue at the points where the sticks overlap. The glue will bind them together well. When you make a frame, use the inside corner of a box to align the first two sticks. That way you will be sure to glue the first two sticks at a good square angle. Then attach the other two sides.

You Will Need

- **49 straight Popsicle sticks**
- **wood glue**
- **black construction paper**
- **colored filters (gels) or cellophane: green, red, blue**
- **scissors**
- **straight pin**
- **masking tape or black tape**
- **ruler**

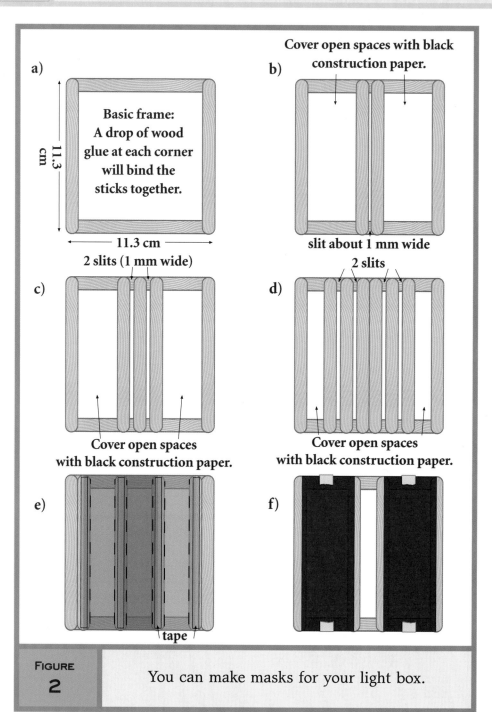

a)

11.3 cm

**Basic frame:
A drop of wood
glue at each corner
will bind the
sticks together.**

◄──── 11.3 cm ────►

2 slits (1 mm wide)

b)

**Cover open spaces with black
construction paper.**

slit about 1 mm wide

c)

Cover open spaces
with black construction paper.

d)

2 slits

Cover open spaces
with black construction paper.

e)

tape

f)

**FIGURE
2**

You can make masks for your light box.

Your frame should look like the one in Figure 2a. Make nine frames in the same way.

2. Less sturdy masks can be made from heavy black construction paper. If you use construction paper, you will have to use scissors to cut out slits and openings that match the ones in Figure 2.

    The masks that require colored filters (gels) can be made when needed. There are about ten experiments that require these filters. Don't worry if you are not able to obtain them; there are plenty of experiments you can do without them. In fact, colored cellophane can be substituted for the colored filters in several of the experiments that call for colored light. You can do experiments with the other masks while you obtain the colored filters (gels) needed to make the colored masks.

    Sheets of colored light filters, sometimes called color gels, can be purchased from a theatrical supply store, ordered from a science supply company, or purchased through several Internet sites (see Appendix).

    The masks you will need to make for the experiments in this book are listed on the next page.

Pinhole mask: Cut a rectangle the same size as the frame in Figure 2a from heavy black construction paper. Use a pin to make a hole in the center of the paper. Tape the paper to the frame.

Single-slit mask: Add two Popsicle sticks to the frame as shown in Figure 2b. Leave a slit about 1 mm ($^1/_{16}$ in) wide between the two center sticks, which must be very straight. DO NOT use warped sticks! Tape black construction paper over the rest of the mask.

Two-slit mask: Glue a straight Popsicle stick across the center of a third frame. Add another straight Popsicle stick to each side of the center stick. Leave a slit about 1 mm wide on either side of the center stick as shown in Figure 2c. Tape black construction paper to the frame to cover the openings that remain.

Four-slit mask: Glue two straight sticks side-by-side across the center of a fourth frame. There should be no space between them (see Figure 2d). Then glue two more straight sticks on either side of the center sticks creating two 1-mm slits on each side of the center sticks as shown in Figure 2d.

Tape black construction paper over the two wider open spaces that remain.

Three-color mask: Add four Popsicle sticks to the fifth basic frame as shown in Figure 2e. Cover the three open spaces between the sticks with a red, a blue, and a green filter as shown. The colored strips should be about 11 cm long and 2 cm wide. Cut narrow strips of masking or black tape to fasten the sides of the colored filters to the sticks.

Wide-slit mask: Add two Popsicle sticks about 2 cm apart to the central area of a sixth basic frame as shown in Figure 2f. Cover the areas on either side of the wide slit with black construction paper.

Red mask: From a sheet of the red gel, cut a piece of red filter the same size as the seventh basic wood frame. Tape the edges of the colored filter to the frame. Do the same with blue gel and green gel to make two more colored masks.

You can build a light box using a shoe box and a light socket. Different masks will be used to change the light exiting the box.

This is the two-slit mask (Figure 2c).

This is the pinhole mask (Figure 2a).

OTHER MATERIALS YOU WILL NEED

- concave mirror, such as a makeup or shaving mirror
- cylindrical jars or tumblers, small, glass or plastic, with smooth, vertical sides and a base that is not too thick
- dark room
- meterstick, yardstick, or tape measure
- mirrors, two plane (ordinary flat-surfaced) mirrors, preferably small ones (approximately 5 cm x 8 cm [2 in x 3 in]) that reflect light from their front surface (Ordinary glass mirrors with silvered backs reflect light from the rear surface after the light passes through the glass. Touch the mirror with your fingertip. If there is a small space between your fingertip and its image, reflection is at the rear surface. If your fingertip and its image touch, reflection is at the front surface.)
- notebook, pens, and pencils
- plastic container, small, clear, rectangular or square
- prism, glass or plastic
- protractor, preferably one with a straight edge that lies along the 0-180 degree line rather than one in which the straight edge extends slightly beyond the 0-180 degree line
- ruler, 30 cm (12 in)
- white cardboard screen: To make one, tape a sheet of white paper to a cardboard sheet about 30 cm x 25 cm (12 in x 10 in) or use a sheet of white cardboard of the same size.

REFLECTION OF LIGHT, IMAGES, AND SHADOWS

Now that you have built your light box, you can use it to do experiments. You will see the results of the experiments best if you do them in a dark place. The light in your light box should be the only source of light.

In this chapter, you will investigate how light behaves when it bounces off (reflects from) smooth surfaces such as mirrors. You will also discover how images form, how shadows show us that light travels in straight lines, and how the source of light affects shadows.

THE BASIC LAW OF REFLECTION

1. **Be sure the clear bulb** in the light box is turned so that its straight filament is vertical (in an up-down direction) as shown in Figure 1. Cover the side opening in the light box with the single-slit mask. The top of the box can probably be used to hold the mask in place. If not, use small pieces of tape. Darken the room—the darker the better. Then turn on the lightbulb in the light box. You should see a narrow beam of light coming from the box. (We will call the narrow beam a ray of light even though, technically, a light ray has no width.) Lay a sheet of white paper in front of the single slit so you can see the ray clearly on paper.

You Will Need

- tape
- single-slit mask
- light box
- dark room
- white paper
- plane mirror
- protractor
- pencil
- ruler

2. Place a mirror on the light ray. (If possible, use a mirror that reflects light from its front surface.) Put your fingertip against the mirror. If

your fingertip and its image touch, you have a mirror with a front reflecting surface. If there is a small gap between your fingertip and its image, light is reflected at the mirror's rear surface. What happens to the light when it strikes the mirror?

The ray coming to the mirror is called the incident ray. The ray leaving the mirror is called the reflected ray. As you change the angle of the incident ray, what happens to the angle of the reflected ray?

3. Place a protractor against the mirror. If your protractor's edge lies along the 0–180 degree line (Figure 3bi), you can place your mirror against the protractor's straight edge as shown in Figure 3a. Move the mirror and protractor until the incident ray strikes the exact center of the protractor's base. Then you can measure the angle of incidence, which is the angle between the incident ray and the perpendicular line (a line connecting 90° with the center of the protractor's base). And you can measure the angle of reflection (the angle between the reflected ray and the perpendicular line).

If the protractor's 0–180 degree line is slightly above the protractor's edge (Figure 3bii), place the mirror along

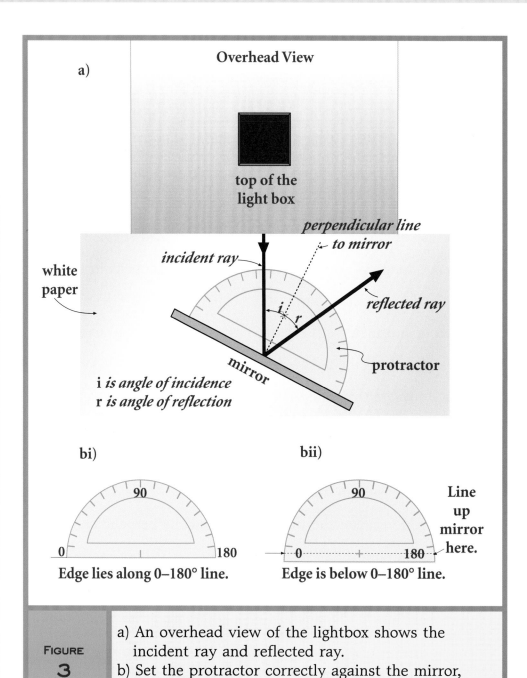

Overhead View

a)

top of the
light box

*perpendicular line
to mirror*

incident ray

white
paper

i *r*

reflected ray

mirror

protractor

i *is angle of incidence*
r *is angle of reflection*

bi)

90

0   180

Edge lies along 0–180° line.

bii)

90

Line
up
mirror
here.

0   180

Edge is below 0–180° line.

FIGURE

3

a) An overhead view of the lightbox shows the
incident ray and reflected ray.
b) Set the protractor correctly against the mirror,
depending on your protractor's 0–180° line.

the 0–180 degree line and measure the angles of incidence and refraction from the line perpendicular to the mirror.

If you are using a mirror with a rear-reflecting surface (see "Other Materials"), start with a large angle of incidence. You will see two reflected rays. The bright ray is reflected from the rear surface. The dimmer ray is reflected from the glass on the front surface. Use the dimmer ray to measure the angle of reflection. When you measure smaller angles of incidence, be sure to look for the much dimmer reflected ray.

4. Change the angle of incidence several times so that you measure both large and small angles of incidence. In each case, measure both the angle of incidence and the angle of reflection. How do these two angles compare? What can you conclude about the angle of reflection for any angle of incidence?

WHERE IS THE IMAGE IN A PLANE MIRROR?

When you look in a plane (flat) **mirror,** you see your reflected image. Your image appears to be behind the mirror. But is it really where it appears to be?

1. To find out, you can use a technique called parallax. It involves looking at something from two different angles. To see how it works, hold one finger at arm's length in front of your face. Hold the other finger close to your face. Now look at both fingers, first with your right eye and then with your left eye. As you can see, the position of the nearer finger shifts a lot relative to the distant finger.

2. Now hold one finger on top of the other at an arm's length in front of your face. Again, close first one eye and then the other. This time the two fingers stay together. They do not shift relative to one another. There is no parallax between them, but there is parallax between the two fingers and more distant objects.

You Will Need

- **small plane mirror**
- **table**
- **clay**
- **2 pencils**
- **ruler**

3. Lack of parallax can be used to locate the image you see in a mirror. Stand a small mirror upright on a table. You may need a piece of clay to support the mirror. Use a piece of clay to support a pencil about 10 cm (4 in) in front of the mirror as shown in Figure 4. Support a second pencil in the same way behind the mirror.

4. Put your head behind the pencil in front of the mirror. You can see the entire pencil in front of the mirror, its image in the mirror, and the top of the second pencil behind the

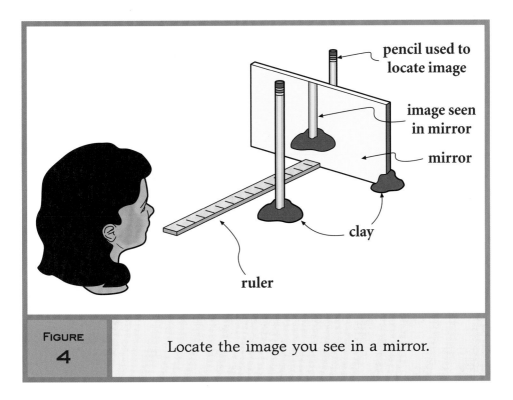

pencil used to locate image

image seen in mirror

mirror

clay

ruler

FIGURE 4

Locate the image you see in a mirror.

mirror. Move the pencil behind the mirror to different positions, keeping it in line with the image of the pencil in front of the mirror. At each position, look first with your right eye and then with your left eye. When there is no parallax (the image and the pencil behind the mirror stick together no matter which eye sees them), you know the pencil behind the mirror is at the same place as the image of the pencil you see in the mirror.

5. Measure the distance from the mirror to the pencil in front of the mirror and from the mirror to the pencil behind the mirror. How do these distances compare?

6. Repeat the experiment several times with the pencil at different distances from the mirror. What can you conclude about the apparent location of the pencil's image? What does this experiment tell you about the apparent location of your image when you look into a plane mirror?

IDEA FOR YOUR SCIENCE FAIR

Early Greek scholars believed that we see because light rays come out of our eyes, strike objects, and reflect back to our eyes. Design an experiment to show that light does not come out of our eyes.

1. **You can use your light box** to make a simple model to show how a plane mirror forms images. Cover the opening in your light box with the two-slit mask. Lay a sheet of white paper in front of the mask. Darken the room and turn on the light-bulb.

2. Ask a partner to use a mirror to reflect one of the rays so that the two rays cross as shown in Figure 5a. The point where the two rays cross can represent a point on an object (O) from which two light rays emerge. Reflect these two rays from a second mirror as shown in Figure 5b. Notice how the two reflected rays diverge (spread out) after being reflected.

You Will Need

- **light box**
- **two-slit mask**
- **white paper**
- **a partner**
- **2 mirrors**
- **ruler**
- **pencil**
- **dark room**
- **colored filter or colored cellophane**

3. Use a ruler and pencil to draw lines along the rays reflected from the second mirror. Next, draw a line along the front of the second mirror, which

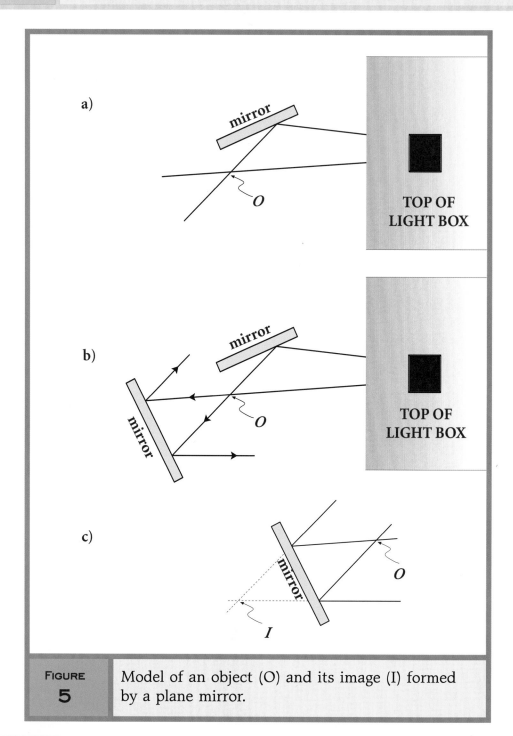

you used to reflect the two rays. Remove the mirror. Then use your ruler and pencil to make dotted lines extending the two reflected rays back to a point where they meet behind the mirror (Figure 5c).

4. Measure the distance from the line where the mirror was located to the point behind the mirror where the extended rays meet. That point represents the position of the image (I) where the two reflected rays appeared to be coming from. How do the distances from object (O) to mirror and from image (I) to mirror compare?

The model shows two light rays coming from a point on an object. The rays are reflected to form just one point on an image that appears to be behind the mirror. With real objects, every point on the object sends out countless rays. But the principle is the same for many points as it is for one point with two rays. All the rays that strike the mirror from all the many points on the object are reflected to form an image that appears to be behind the mirror. Rays of light from all the points on the object are reflected and appear to be coming from behind the mirror. The image is called a virtual image because it only appears to be behind the mirror.

5. Look at yourself in a mirror. Wink your right eye. Which eye does your image wink? To see why your mirror image seems to be reversed right for left, again cover the opening in your light box with the two-slit mask. Put a strip of colored filter or cellophane over one of the slits. Use a mirror to reflect one of the rays so that the two rays cross to form a point that represents a point on an object as before. Now look in the mirror. Notice that if the colored ray came from the right side of the object, it seems to come from the left side of the image. Or if it came from the left side of the object, it appears to come from the right side of the image.

IDEA FOR YOUR SCIENCE FAIR

Try to print a message that can be read by holding it up to a mirror. Show how Leonardo DaVinci used this method to record his laboratory notes.

A THIRD AND DIFFERENT IMAGE

1. **Stand two mirrors upright** and at right angles (90°) to each other near the edge of a table. Look into the mirrors with your face between them. You will see three images of your face. Account for each image. Wink your right eye. Which eye does each image wink? What is different about the middle image? Why is it different?

2. Lay a sheet of white paper in front of the opening in your light box. Stand two mirrors upright and at a right angle to each other on the paper. You may need clay to support the mirrors.

3. Cover the opening in the light box with the two-slit mask. Cover one slit with a strip of a colored light filter or cellophane. This will help you identify rays. Darken the room and turn on the lightbulb in the light box.

4. Use a third mirror to reflect

You Will Need

- **3 mirrors**
- **sheet of white paper**
- **light box**
- **clay**
- **two-slit mask**
- **strip of colored light filter or colored cellophane**
- **dark room**

one of the light rays coming from the light box so that the rays cross. The point where they cross can represent a point (O) on an object. Have the rays reflect off both mirrors as shown in Figure 6. Where would the image caused by the double reflection of the rays appear to be located? To find out, look at the dotted lines used to project the two twice-reflected rays to a point where they appear to meet. (This is the same method you used to locate an image in a single mirror [Figure 5c].)

Two other images would be formed by the single reflection of rays coming from the object—the images seen by

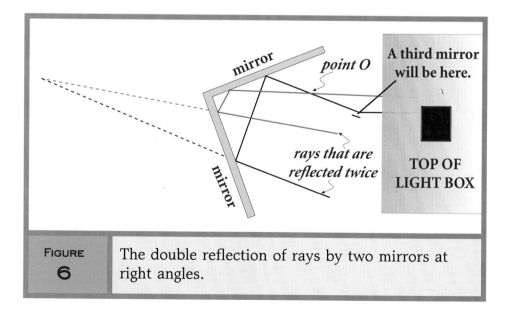

FIGURE 6 The double reflection of rays by two mirrors at right angles.

looking into either mirror. Where would these images be located?

IDEA FOR YOUR SCIENCE FAIR

Explain why you see three images when you look into two mirrors at right angles to one another. Then use diagrams of reflected rays to explain why the middle image is not reversed right for left as images in a plane mirror usually are.

MANY IMAGES

1. **Lay a sheet of white paper** in front of the light-box opening. Stand two mirrors upright with their reflective surfaces facing each other as shown in Figure 7a. Use small lumps of clay to support the mirrors. Hold a pencil upright between the two mirrors. Then look into one of the mirrors. Describe what you see.

2. To explain the many images, darken the room, cover the opening in the light box with the single-slit mask, and turn on the lightbulb in the light box. Stand the two mirrors upright on the paper. The mirrors should be parallel, with their reflective surfaces facing each other. Use a third mirror to reflect the single ray of light onto one of the mirrors. Try to have the reflected ray strike one of the parallel mirrors as nearly perpendicular as possible. See Figure 7b.

You Will Need

- **3 mirrors (2 long, 1 short)**
- **clay**
- **pencil**
- **sheet of white paper**
- **light box**
- **single-slit mask**
- **dark room**
- **hallway or room with large mirrors on opposite walls**

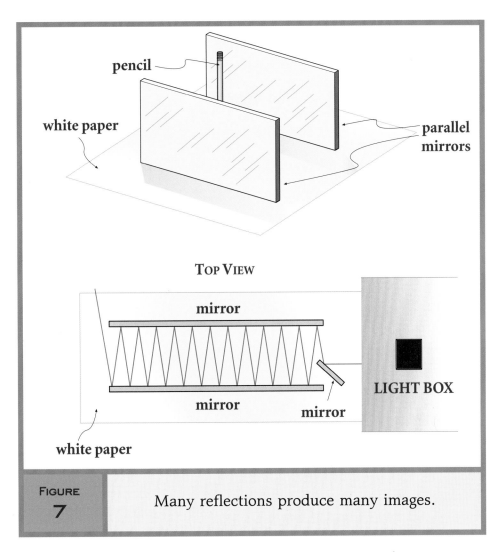

FIGURE 7 Many reflections produce many images.

How many back-and-forth reflections can you make?

3. To see many images on a larger scale, find a hallway or room with large mirrors on opposite walls. Stand between the mirrors. How many images of yourself can you see? Explain why the images seem to get farther and farther away.

REFLECTION AND A CONCAVE MIRROR

1. **Concave mirrors bow inward** like a shallow dish. To see how they reflect light from a distant object, tape a strip of aluminum foil about 4 cm wide and 10 cm long to the lower outside of a small glass or plastic jar. The foil should go about halfway around the jar. Be sure the foil is very tight and smooth. The foil on the jar makes a concave mirror. Find a jar cover with a diameter slightly smaller than the diameter of the jar that holds the foil. The smaller jar cover

You Will Need

- **AN ADULT**
- **aluminum foil**
- **ruler**
- **small glass or plastic jar**
- **jar cover from a slightly smaller jar**
- **tape**
- **white paper**
- **light box**
- **two-slit mask**

- **concave mirror, such as a makeup or shaving mirror**
- **a partner**
- **white cardboard or white paper taped to cardboard to make a screen**
- **meterstick, yardstick, or tape measure**
- **matches**
- **candle**
- **dark room**

should have a light-colored top surface. If it doesn't, cut a circle from a sheet of white paper and tape it to the cover. Drop the cover into the larger jar, white side up.

2. Let light from your light box pass through a two-slit mask. Place the jar with the foil on the two rays. Look at the reflected rays on the cover you dropped into the larger jar. Notice how the reflected rays converge (come together).

3. Since a concave mirror brings light rays from a distant source together, we might expect a concave mirror to form images. To see if this is true, hold a concave mirror, such as a makeup or shaving mirror, several meters or yards from a window. Turn the mirror toward distant objects (**not the sun**) that you can see through the window. Have a partner hold a white cardboard screen in front of the mirror.

4. Have your partner move the cardboard screen toward and away from the mirror. You will find a point at which an image of the distant objects forms on the screen. Is the image right side up or inverted? The point where the light rays come together to form an image of distant objects is the focal point of the mirror. Measure the distance between the mirror and the cardboard screen. That distance is the

focal length of the mirror. It is the point where parallel rays are brought together. (You will see why these rays are parallel when you do Experiment 2-9.) What is the approximate focal length of your concave mirror?

The images made by a concave mirror are not virtual images like the ones you saw in a plane mirror. As you can see, the image on the cardboard screen is really there. For that reason, such images are called real images.

5. Will a concave mirror form real images of nearer objects? To find out, **ask an adult** to light a candle in a dark room. Hold the concave mirror about two focal lengths from the candle. Can a partner locate the real image of the candle flame using the white cardboard screen to "capture" the image? What do you notice about the image?

6. Move the mirror farther from the candle. Where is the image now? How has its size changed? What happens to the size and location of the image as you move the mirror closer to the candle? What happens when you place the mirror less than one focal length from the candle? Can you find a real image?

7. Hold the mirror less than one focal length from your face.

Look at your image. How does the size of your image compare with the size of your face?

The image you see when you hold a concave mirror less than one focal length from an object is a virtual image. It is similar to the images you see in a plane mirror but larger. It appears to be where it is because your eye assumes that the

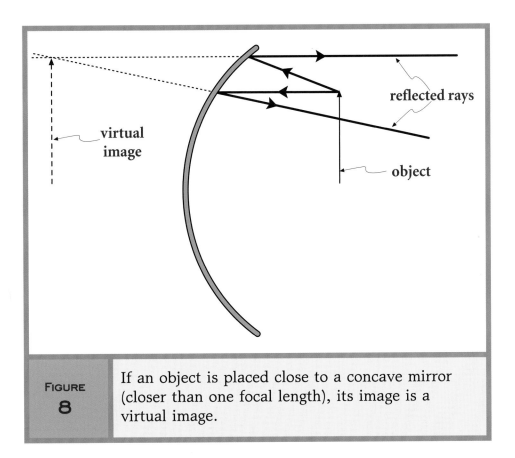

virtual image

reflected rays

object

FIGURE 8   If an object is placed close to a concave mirror (closer than one focal length), its image is a virtual image.

diverging rays originate where they appear to join at a point behind the mirror, as shown in Figure 8.

IDEAS FOR YOUR SCIENCE FAIR

- Design and carry out an experiment to show that light rays from distant objects can be considered to be parallel.

- The surface of convex mirrors, such as the kind found on the right-hand side of automobiles, bulge outward like the backside of a spoon. Obtain a convex mirror and examine the images it forms. Are the images real or virtual? Are they right side up or inverted? How does the size of the images they form compare with the size of the objects from which they originate?

1. **Mirrors are not the only place** where images form. To see that this is true, cover the opening in your light box with the pinhole mask. Darken the room and turn on the light box. Hold a white cardboard screen in front of the mask. You will see an image of the bulb's filament on the screen. What happens to the size of the image as you move the screen farther from the pinhole? Closer to the pinhole?

2. Is the image upright or is it inverted like the real images made by a concave mirror? To find out, open a large paper clip so that it forms a right angle (90°). Put the paper clip inside the hole in the cover. Slowly move the horizontal part

You Will Need

- **AN ADULT** !
- **light box**
- **pinhole mask**
- **dark room**
- **white cardboard screen**
- **large paper clip**
- **box about 30 cm x 45 cm (12 in x 18 in)**

- **candle and candle holder**
- **sharp knife**
- **tape**
- **black construction paper**
- **pin**
- **matches**

of the paper clip up and down in front of the bulb. Watch the shadow of the paper clip move across the image. What can you conclude?

3. Is the image reversed right for left? To find out, turn the bulb 90° so that its filament is horizontal. How does the image change? Move the vertical part of the paper clip slowly back and forth in front of the bulb. Which way does the paper clip's shadow move? Is the pinhole image reversed right for left?

4. Here is another way to make a pinhole image. Find a box about 30 cm x 45 cm (12 in x 18 in). Discard the cover and place the box on its end in front of a candle. In the box, cut a small square hole that is slightly higher than the top of the candle. Tape a piece of black construction paper over the hole. Make a pinhole in the paper (see Figure 9a).

5. **Ask an adult** to light the candle. Hold your white cardboard screen on the opposite side of the pinhole from the candle as shown in Figure 9a. Look at the image of the candle flame. Is it right side up or inverted? What happens to the size of the image as you move the screen farther from the pinhole? Closer to the pinhole?

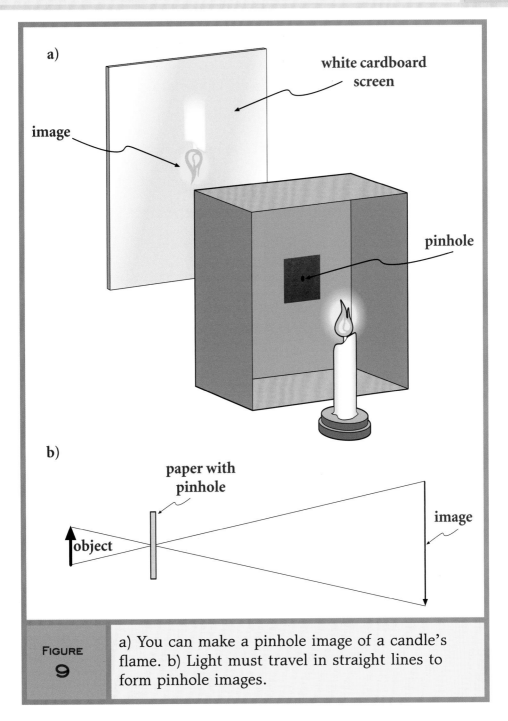

a)

white cardboard screen

image

pinhole

b)

paper with pinhole

object

image

FIGURE 9 a) You can make a pinhole image of a candle's flame. b) Light must travel in straight lines to form pinhole images.

What do you think will happen if you add a second pinhole? A third? A few pinholes? Does the size of the pinhole affect the image? If it does, how does it affect it? Does the shape of the pinhole affect the image? For instance, will the image made by a tiny square hole be different than the image made by a round hole of the same width?

As Figure 9b shows, light must travel in straight lines to form a pinhole image. In the next experiment, you will discover additional evidence that light travels in straight lines.

1. **Remove the cover from the light box.** Then turn the light box on its side. Turn the bulb so the end of the filament is facing you. The end of the filament is now a point of light. Hold your hand between the point of light and a wall. Look at the shadow of your hand on the wall. Move your hand closer to the light. What happens to the size of its shadow? What happens to its size as you move your hand farther from the light? Where must you hold your hand to make it cast the smallest shadow?

2. Place the white cardboard screen exactly 1 meter or 1 yard from the point of

You Will Need

- **light box**
- **dark room**
- **white cardboard screen**
- **meterstick or yardstick**
- **a partner**
- **forceps**
- **cardboard**
- **ruler**
- **paper and pencil**
- **block of wood**
- **jar lid**
- **metal can**
- **cone-shaped object**
- **tennis ball**
- **large (1 m x 1m or 1 yd x 1 yd) sheet of cardboard**
- **60-watt frosted lightbulb**

light. Have a partner use forceps to hold a square piece of cardboard, 5 cm (2 in) on a side, halfway (50 cm or 18 in) between the end of the filament and the screen. Measure the square's shadow. How does it compare with the size of the cardboard square casting the shadow?

3. Make a sketch to show how you think the shadow is formed. Then predict the size of the shadow you will see when your partner holds the cardboard square one-fourth of the way (25 cm or 9 in) from the point of light to the screen. Measure the shadow. Was your prediction correct?

4. Find a rectangular object, such as a block of wood, and a circular object, such as a jar lid. Use these objects to cast rectangular and circular shadows on the screen or wall. What other shadow shapes can you make using the rectangular object? Can you make a square shadow? A trapezoidal shadow?

5. What other shadow shapes can you make using the circular object? Can you make an oval shadow? What other shadow shapes can you make with the circle?

6. Find a cylinder, such as a metal can. Can you make a rectangular shadow with the cylinder? Can you make a circular

shadow. What other shadow shapes can you make with the cylinder?

7. What shadow shapes can you make with a cone-shaped object?

8. What is the shape of the only shadow you can make with a sphere such as a tennis ball?

9. Using the bulb in your light box as a point source of light, cast a shadow of your partner's profile on a screen made from a very large piece of cardboard. Where should your partner sit to make a large shadow profile? To make a small shadow profile?

   If you cover the screen with a large sheet of paper, you can trace a profile and then cut it out.

10. Make shadow profiles using sunlight. Can you change the size of a shadow profile using sunlight? What does this tell you about the light rays reaching the earth from the sun?

11. Return the light box to its normal position. Turn on the light in the light box. Be sure the filament is in its normal vertical position. Leave the side opening opposite the lightbulb uncovered. Lay a sheet of white paper in front of the opening.

Hold a pencil upright in front of the opening. Notice the sharp shadow cast by the pencil.

12. Turn the bulb in the light box so that the filament is horizontal. Again, stand the pencil upright in front of the opening. What is different about the pencil's shadow? Why do you think the shadow is different?

13. Turn off the bulb. While it is cooling, make drawings to explain the shadow's appearance for each arrangement of the bulb's filament.

14. Now that the bulb has cooled, replace it with a 60-watt frosted bulb. Try to predict what the shadow of the pencil will look like when you again hold the pencil upright and turn on the bulb. Look at the shadow. Did you predict correctly? If not, having seen the shadow, can you now explain its appearance?

IDEAS FOR YOUR SCIENCE FAIR

- Examine shadows cast by light sources other than a point source. You might try a fluorescent bulb, showcase bulb, spotlight, or flashlight. How do the shadows differ? Try to explain why they are different.

- How can you make more than one shadow of the same object?

- Look at shadows cast by the sun. Is the sun a point source of light? What evidence can you use to answer this question?

- Can shadows be reflected? Do an experiment to find out.

LIGHT, SHADOWS, AND DISTANCE

If **you made shadow profiles** using sunlight in the previous experiment, you probably found that you could not change the size of the profile. In this experiment you will see why you couldn't.

1. Turn the light box on its side. Then turn the bulb so that the end of the filament is a point of light as you look at it.

2. Stick 3 pins into a piece of cardboard about 30 cm (1 ft) square. The pins should be near one edge of the cardboard, upright, and side by side about 2 centimeters (1 inch) apart.

3. Hold the cardboard close to the light. You will see that the pins' shadows spread apart. Now slowly move the cardboard away from the point of light. What happens to the shadows? Do they become parallel or nearly so? What does this tell you about the light rays coming from the light? How does distance affect the light rays that reach you from a light source?

4. Take the cardboard out into sunlight. Let the

You Will Need

- **light box**
- **3 pins**
- **cardboard (about 30 cm x 30 cm or 12 in x 12 in)**
- **ruler**
- **sunlight**

sun cast shadows of the pins on the cardboard. Are the pins' shadows parallel or do they spread apart? What does this tell you about light from the sun?

IDEA FOR YOUR SCIENCE FAIR

Look at the shadow of a tall object that is cast by the sun. Notice that the end of the shadow is fuzzy, but the shadow close to the object is sharp. The sun actually covers about half a degree of the sky, so it is not a perfect point source of light. Use this information to explain why the end of the shadow is fuzzy.

LIGHT INTENSITY (BRIGHTNESS)

You know from experience that a light looks dimmer (less intense) as you move away from it. Imagine how much brighter the Sun would look if you were on the planet Mercury rather than Earth. Mercury is approximately 58 million kilometers (36 million miles) from the Sun. The distance from the Sun to Earth is approximately 150 million kilometers (93 million miles). The Sun would look even dimmer on Mars, which is about 228 million kilometers (142 million miles) from the Sun. Certain stars, which are known to be much brighter than the Sun, can barely be seen because they are so far away.

If you double your distance from a lightbulb, does the bulb's light become half as intense (bright)? You can do a simple experiment that will give you the answer.

You Will Need

- **AN ADULT** ⛔
- **light box**
- **sharp knife**
- **ruler**
- **2 large (30 cm x 30 cm or 12 in x 12 in) sheets of cardboard**
- **pen or pencil**
- **dark room**
- **a partner**

1. Turn the light box on its side. Turn the bulb so that you see its filament as a point of light. **Have an adult** use a sharp knife to cut out a square 3 cm (1 in) on a side from the center of a large (30 cm x 30 cm or 12 in x 12 in) sheet of cardboard.

2. On another sheet of cardboard, draw a square that is 12 cm x 12 cm (4 in x 4 in). Divide that big square into 16 smaller squares each 3 cm (1 in) on a side.

3. Darken the room and turn on the lightbulb in the light box. Have a partner hold the cardboard with the small (3 cm x

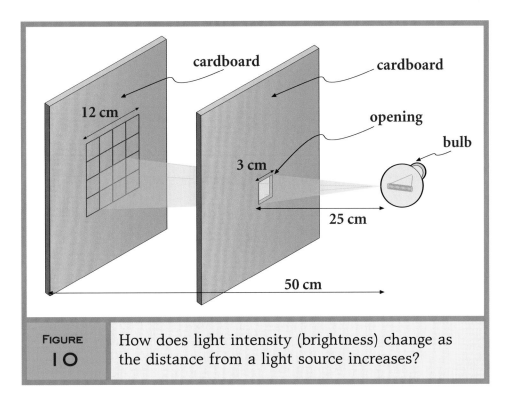

| FIGURE 10 | How does light intensity (brightness) change as the distance from a light source increases? |

3 cm) square opening exactly 25 cm (10 in) from the end of the bright filament (the point of light). Hold the other sheet of cardboard twice as far (50 cm, or 20 in) from the light as shown in Figure 10. How many 3-cm x 3-cm (1-in x 1-in) squares does the light cover on the sheet you are holding? What is the intensity of the light twice as far from its source?

If the intensity is half as much, the light should cover twice as much area, which would be a square about 4.2 cm (or 1 $\frac{7}{16}$ in) on a side. Is the intensity half as much? Or is it one-fourth as much? It is one-fourth as much if it covers four times as much area, which would be four squares on your screen, or a square 6 cm or 2 in on each side.

Can you predict how many squares the light will cover when you move your sheet to a point 75 cm from the end of the filament? What do you find? Has the intensity of the light become one-third as much or one-ninth as much?

How many squares does the light cover when you move your sheet to a point 100 cm from the point of light? Is the intensity one-fourth as great or one-sixteenth as great?

What can you conclude about the way the intensity of light changes as the distance from the light increases?

REFRACTION: THE BENDING OF LIGHT

You have seen that light travels in straight lines. However, it does sometimes change direction. When light changes direction, or bends, we say it is refracted. In this chapter, you will find several ways to refract light. You can make it bend with water, glass, and plastic. Lenses and prisms bend light, and so does your eye. Refraction allows you to see.

BENDING LIGHT

1. **Darken the room** and turn on the lightbulb in your light box. Cover the opening in your light box with the single-slit mask. Lay a sheet of white paper in front of the mask.

2. Place a small, clear, rectangular or square plastic container on the narrow light beam coming from the light box. Add water to the container until it is three-quarters full. You can also use a glass or plastic block or make one by stacking glass or plastic microscope slides side by side.

3. Turn the container or glass block so that the light hits the box or block at a sharp angle as shown in Figure 11a. Notice how the light is bent (refracted) as it enters and leaves the water or block. Are the beams parallel as they enter and leave the water? Is all the light that hits the water refracted or is some of it reflected?

4. Place a jar of water on the beam. Does the light

You Will Need

- **light box**
- **dark room**
- **single-slit mask**
- **a small, clear, rectangular or square plastic container or glass or plastic block**
- **water**
- **glass or plastic jar**
- **glass or plastic prism**

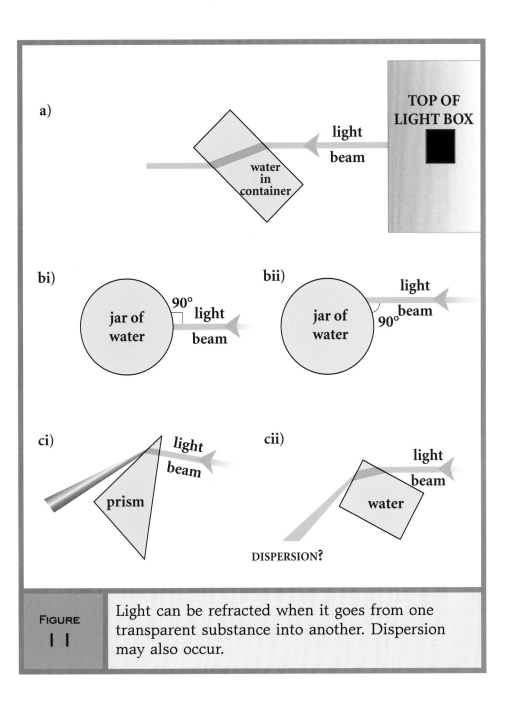

a)

light beam

TOP OF LIGHT BOX

water in container

bi)

jar of water

90° light beam

bii)

jar of water

90° light beam

ci)

light beam

prism

cii)

light beam

water

DISPERSION?

FIGURE 11

Light can be refracted when it goes from one transparent substance into another. Dispersion may also occur.

bend if it hits the very middle of the jar at an incident angle of 90 degrees (Figure 11bi)? Will it bend if it hits at a lesser angle (to one side of the middle of the jar [as shown in Figure 11bii])?

5. Repeat the experiment using a glass or plastic prism as shown in Figure 11ci. Is light refracted by the prism? If you bend the light enough, you can turn the refracted beam into a band of colors. Look carefully at the colors. Which color is refracted the most? The least? The spreading of the refracted light into different colors is called dispersion. Where have you seen dispersion in the natural world?

6. Can you cause dispersion of white light by having it enter the corner of a container of water at a sharp angle, as shown in Figure 11cii?

IDEAS FOR YOUR SCIENCE FAIR

- Which bends light more, glass or water? Design and carry out an experiment to find out.

- Using a second prism, see if you can recombine the dispersed colors to make white light.

BENDING LIGHT WITH A CONVEX LENS

We see things because light emitted by or reflected from those things reaches our eyes. In an open space, we can see the same thing no matter where we stand. This tells us that the light from the object is emitted or reflected in all directions. A convex lens, such as a magnifying glass, can refract light. It can bend light so that light coming from every point on an object can be brought back together to form similar points. It can, therefore, bend and bring back together light from all the points on an object to form an image of the object. This is what the

You Will Need

- **AN ADULT** !
- **convex lens, such as a magnifying glass**
- **room with a window**
- **60-watt frosted bulb**
- **light box**
- **matches**
- **candle**
- **dark room**
- **a partner**
- **white cardboard screen**
- **plastic sandwich bag**
- **basic mask frame**
- **Magic Marker**

lenses in a camera, microscope, or telescope do to form images. Let's see that this is true.

1. Hold a convex lens near a wall on the opposite side of a room from a window. Move the lens closer to and farther from the wall until you see a clear image on the wall. This a real image. The image is really on the wall. It is not a virtual image like the kind you see in a plane mirror. Is the image right side up or upside down?

2. **Ask an adult** to light a candle in a dark room. Hold the convex lens a meter (yard) or so from the candle. Ask a partner to hold a white cardboard screen on the other side of the lens from the candle. Have your partner move the cardboard screen until a clear image of the candle appears on the screen.

3. Move the lens closer to the candle. How does this affect the size of the image? How does it affect the distance between the lens and a clear image?

4. Move the lens farther from the candle. How does this affect the size of the image? How does it affect the distance between the lens and a clear image?

5. To make a simpler image, replace the bulb in the light box with a 60-watt frosted bulb. Put the cover back on the light

box. Then pull a plastic sandwich bag over a basic mask frame. Using a Magic Marker, draw an upright arrow on the plastic at the center of the mask. Put the mask with the arrow over the opening in the light box.

6. Darken the room and turn on the lightbulb in the light box. Hold the white cardboard screen and a convex lens in front of the arrow. Move the lens and cardboard screen different distances from the mask until you get a sharp image of the arrow on the cardboard screen. Is the image upside down? How can you test to see if the image is reversed right for left?

7. If you move the lens farther from the arrow, what happens to the size of the arrow's image? What happens to the distance between the lens and the cardboard screen? What happens if you move the lens closer to the arrow? Is the image bigger? Is the distance between the lens and the cardboard screen greater? If you hold the lens very close to the arrow, can you still make an image?

IDEA FOR YOUR SCIENCE FAIR

How do you think a concave lens bends light? Do an experiment to find out.

A MODEL OF A CONVEX LENS

You can use your **light box** and a water-filled glass or plastic jar to make a model of a convex lens. The model will help you see how a lens refracts light to make images. Be sure the clear bulb is in your light box and that the filament is in a vertical position.

1. Cover the opening in the light box with the two-slit mask, darken the room, and turn on the lightbulb in the light box. Lay a long sheet of white paper in front of the mask. Then put the jar of water on the two narrow light beams coming through the mask. The jar of water is a model of a convex lens. What happens to the light rays as they enter and leave the jar?

2. You can make a better model to show how a lens forms an image. Use

You Will Need

- **light box**
- **glass or plastic jar representing a model of a convex lens**
- **two-slit mask**
- **dark room**
- **long sheet of white paper (tape two sheets together)**
- **water**
- **plane mirror**
- **large comb or hair pick**

a plane mirror, as shown in Figure 12a, to reflect one of the rays so that it crosses the other ray. The point where the two rays cross can represent a point on an object. The two rays coming from that point can represent two rays of light coming from a point on an object. Next, place the jar of water on the two rays a few centimeters from their origin as shown in Figure 12b.

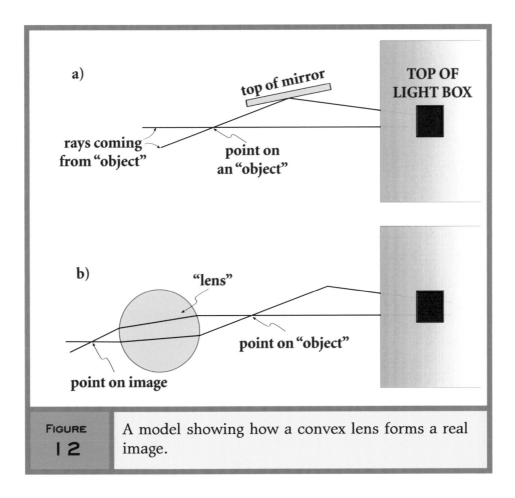

| FIGURE 12 | A model showing how a convex lens forms a real image. |

You can see that the two rays are brought together to form a point. That point represents a point on the image formed by the lens.

3. If you move the "lens" closer to the point representing the object, what happens to the distance between the "image" and the "lens"? What happens if you slowly move the "lens" closer to the "object"? At some point, you will find that the rays coming from the "lens" are parallel. What happens if you move the "lens" still closer to the "object"?

4. To see many rays of light refracted by a lens, replace the mask with a large hair comb or pick (a comb with long tines). Place the "lens" several centimeters (inches) in front of the comb. Notice how the rays bend as they enter and leave the "lens."

IDEA FOR YOUR SCIENCE FAIR

Build a model to show how a concave lens bends light and produces images.

FOCAL LENGTH OF A CONVEX LENS

The **focal point** of a convex lens is the point where parallel rays entering the lens come together. The focal length of a convex lens is the distance from the center of the lens to the focal point. You can find the focal length of the model you used in the previous experiment and the focal length of the real convex lens you used in Experiment 3-2.

1. Cover the opening in the light box with the two-slit mask. Lay a long sheet of white paper in front of the mask. Nearly fill the jar you used in Experiment 3-3 with water.

2. Darken the room and turn on the lightbulb in the light box. Then put the jar on the two narrow light beams coming through the mask. The jar is a model of a convex lens. Use a mirror to

You Will Need

- **light box**
- **two-slit mask**
- **long sheet of white paper**
- **plastic or glass jar used in Experiment 3-3**
- **water**
- **dark room**
- **mirror**
- **pencil**
- **ruler**
- **convex lens**
- **a wall opposite a window**

reflect one of the light rays so that the two rays entering the jar are parallel. Use a pencil to mark the point where the two rays come together (cross) on the other side of the jar. That point is the focal point.

3. Draw a circle around the jar to mark the position of the lens. Then remove the jar. Measure the distance from the center of the circle to the focal point. That distance is the focal length of the lens.

4. To find the focal length of the real convex lens, you can use what you learned in Experiment 2-9. In that experiment you found that light rays from a distant light source can be considered to be parallel.

5. To find the focal length of the real lens, all you need to do is capture the image of a distant object on a wall. Hold a convex lens near a wall opposite a window. Move the lens closer to and farther from the wall until you see a clear image of distant objects on the wall. The clear image is where all the rays coming from each point on the distant objects are brought back together. It is, therefore, the focal point of the light coming from all the points on the distant objects.

6. Measure the distance from the center of the lens to the wall.

That distance is the focal length of the convex lens you are using. What is it?

IDEAS FOR YOUR SCIENCE FAIR

* Measure the focal lengths of several different convex lenses. How is focal length related to the convexity (curvature) of the lenses?

* How would you find the focal point of a concave lens? Why is it often called a virtual focal point?

A BETTER MODEL OF A CONVEX LENS

1. **Cover the opening** in the light box with the four-slit mask. Darken the room and turn on the lightbulb in the light box.

2. Have a partner help you use two mirrors to reflect the two outside light rays. The rays should cross the two inside rays as shown in Figure 13a. Each point where the rays cross represents the end point of an "object." Next, place a jar of water on the rays as shown in Figure 13b. The jar of water represents the convex lens. Notice how the rays come together on the other side of the "lens." The points where those rays cross represent the end points of the "image" of the "object." The "image" may be easier to see if you slightly lift the paper beyond the jar.

3. To see that the image is inverted, cover the two slits on one side of the mask with a strip of a color filter as shown in Figure 13c. You can use the same filter you used

You Will Need

- **light box**
- **four-slit mask**
- **dark room**
- **a partner**
- **2 mirrors**
- **jar or glass of water**
- **white paper**
- **strip of red plastic filter**
- **tape**

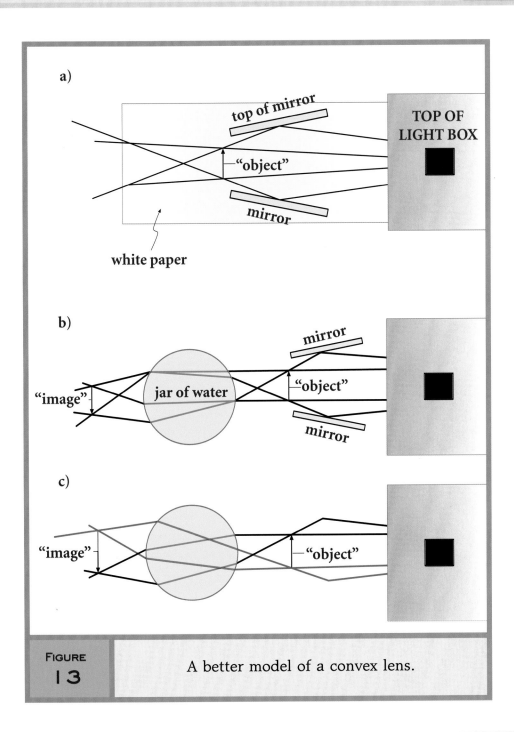

to make the three-color mask. Again, the "image" may be easier to see if you lift the paper beyond the jar.

4. By slowly moving the "lens" closer to the "object," you can make the rays leaving the "lens" become parallel. What happens if you move the "lens" even closer to the "object"? Where is the image now? You can answer that question by doing the next experiment.

USING A CONVEX LENS AS A MAGNIFYING GLASS

1. **Put a convex lens** on some print on this page. Slowly lift the lens. How does the size of the print appear to change? Why is a convex lens sometimes called a magnifying glass or reading glass?

2. You can use your light box to understand how a convex lens can make things look larger. Cover the light-box opening with the two-slit mask. Then darken the room and turn on the lightbulb in the light box. Use a mirror to reflect one of the rays to form a point on an "object" as you did in Experiments 2-3 and 3-3. Move the "lens" (the jar of water) close to the point of light so the rays passing through the lens diverge (spread apart) as shown in Figure 14a.

   As you can see, the rays coming out the far side of

 You Will Need

- **convex lens**
- **light box**
- **two-slit mask**
- **dark room**
- **plane mirrors**
- **jar or glass of water**
- **four-slit mask**
- **red filter used in Experiment 3-5**
- **pen or pencil**
- **white paper**
- **ruler**

the lens do not meet. Instead, they diverge (spread apart). As the projected dotted lines show, the rays seem to be coming from within the "lens." What kind of an image is the magnified image you saw when the convex lens was close to the print? (Hint: Remember the images you saw in a plane mirror [Experiments 2-2 and 2-3].)

3. To make an even better model of the convex lens used as a magnifier, replace the two-slit mask with the four-slit mask. Cover one set of slits with the red filter or cellophane you used in Experiment 3-5. Put white paper on the table surface. Reflect the outside rays with mirrors to make the end points of an object as you did before. Draw a small arrow on the paper to represent the "object." Again, place the lens very close to the "object" as shown in Figure 14b. Notice how the rays diverge after passing through the lens.

4. To locate the virtual "image" of this object, use a sharp pencil or pen to make several dashes on the paper along each diverging ray. Then remove the lens and use a ruler to connect the dashes and extend those rays back toward the lens until they meet. The points where they meet will give you the apparent location of the ends of the image. How does the

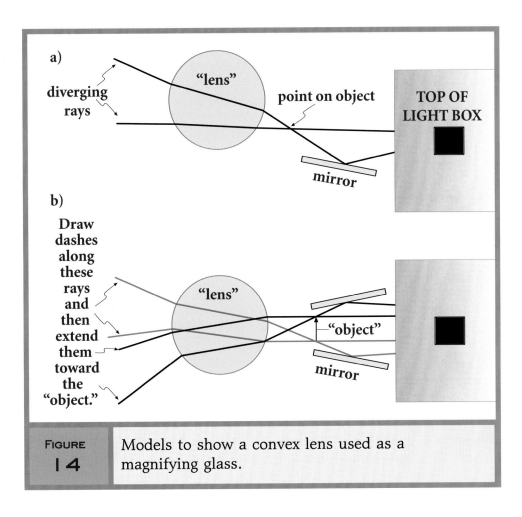

a)

diverging rays

"lens"

point on object

TOP OF LIGHT BOX

mirror

b)

Draw dashes along these rays and then extend them toward the "object."

"lens"

"object"

mirror

| FIGURE 14 | Models to show a convex lens used as a magnifying glass. |

size of the image compare with the size of the object? Is the image right side up or inverted? What kind of an image did you see when you used the convex lens as a magnifier?

IDEAS FOR YOUR SCIENCE FAIR

- What kind of images, real or virtual, would you expect to find using a concave lens? Do an experiment to test your prediction. Then figure out a way to locate the images seen through a concave lens.

- Design and carry out an experiment to locate the images seen through a convex lens used to magnify print.

A MODEL OF THE HUMAN EYE

1. **Look at your eye in a mirror.** The colored part of your eye is called the iris. It is covered by a clear, rounded layer of tissue (the cornea). At the center of the iris is an opening called the pupil. You see it as a dark circle. Light passes into your eye through the pupil. Behind the pupil is a convex lens. Its shape is controlled automatically by muscles. The shape of the lens controls how much light rays bend to form images on the retina at the back of the eye. The retina has nerve cells that respond to light and send signals to the brain, which is where we really see. The lens, together with the cornea and the jellylike fluid inside the eye, bend light to form images on the retina.

2. To make a model of the human eye, begin by covering the opening in the light box with the pinhole mask.

 You Will Need

- **pinhole mask**
- **ruler**
- **spherical (ball-shaped) or nearly spherical glass bowl, vase, or brandy glass**
- **water**
- **light box**
- **magnifying glass**
- **white cardboard screen**
- **dark room**

Enlarge the pinhole until it is about 0.5 cm (¼ in) in diameter. The hole represents the pupil of an eye. In front of the "pupil," place a spherical (ball-shaped) or nearly spherical glass bowl, vase, or brandy glass. Fill the vessel with water. It represents the jellylike fluid that fills most of the eyeball.

3. Darken the room and turn on the lightbulb in the light box. Hold a magnifying glass, which represents the lens in the eye, between the "pupil" and the water. Move the white cardboard screen closer and farther from the water-filled sphere until you see a sharp image of the bulb's filament on the screen. Is the image inverted? How can you find out?

   What does the white screen represent? In what ways is this model not like a real eye?

IDEA FOR YOUR SCIENCE FAIR

Make a model of the human eye that has a lens that can be made more or less convex. Why is this a better model than the one you made in Experiment 3-7? Use your model to show how the human eye adjusts for viewing near and distant objects.

You have probably seen a rainbow in the sky. Rainbows occur when raindrops refract and reflect sunlight. You may have seen a small rainbow when you sprayed water from a garden hose into the air with the sun behind you.

You can make a rainbow using your light box. It won't have a circular shape, but the colors will be there. The rainbow will form because of light refracted by the water and reflected by a mirror in the water. In the natural world, a raindrop refracts sunlight as it enters the drop. Some of the light is reflected from the backside of the drop and then refracted again as the light leaves the drop.

1. Turn the clear bulb in the light box so that the filament is horizontal. Do not turn on the light yet. Put the cover back on. Place a clear plastic container that is about 5 cm (2 in) deep in front of the opening in the light box. Nearly fill the container with water. Put a mirror in

 You Will Need

- **light box**
- **clear plastic container about 5 to 10 cm (2 to 4 in) deep**
- **water**
- **mirror**
- **white cardboard screen**

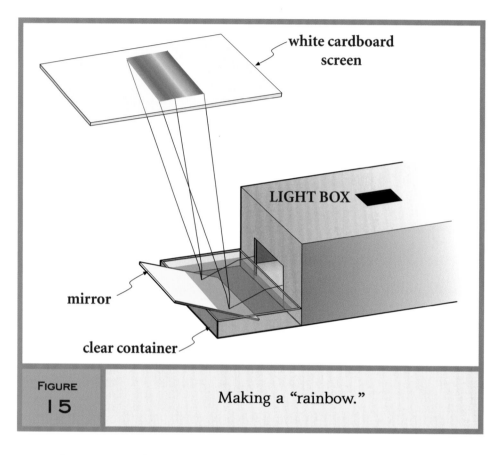

white cardboard
screen

LIGHT BOX

mirror

clear container

| FIGURE 15 | Making a "rainbow." |

the water so that its side rests on the side of the container as shown in Figure 15.

2. Turn on the light. Move the white cardboard screen around above the water until you see a rainbow of colors. As Figure 15 shows, the colors are formed by a three-part process: refraction of the light rays by the water, reflection of the light rays by the mirror, and dispersion of the refracted light into colors.

LIGHT AND COLOR

As you saw in Experiment 3-1, ordinary light, which is called white light, can be separated into colors. We call this property of light *dispersion*. But what happens if we mix different colors of light by adding one color to one or more other colors? You can answer that question by doing the experiments in this chapter.

MIXING LIGHT OF DIFFERENT COLORS

1. **Cover the opening in the light box** with the three-color mask. Lay a sheet of white paper in front of the mask. Be sure the filament of the bulb in the light box is aligned vertically.

2. Darken the room and turn on the lightbulb in the light box. You will see red, blue, and green bands of color on the white paper. Using a mirror, reflect the green light onto the blue light, as shown in Figure 16a. The color you see when those two colors are mixed is called cyan. You might call it blue-green or aqua. The color will vary somewhat depending on how intensely you reflect the green onto the blue. Reflecting the blue onto the green should produce a similar color. (The intensity of a color can be changed by changing the angle of the mirror, reflecting one color onto another closer to or farther from the light box opening, or changing the color that you reflect in order to mix the two colored lights.)

You Will Need

- **light box**
- **three-color mask**
- **white paper**
- **dark room**
- **2 mirrors**

3. Reflect the red light onto the blue light. The color you see when those two colors are mixed is called magenta. You might call it pink or purple. The color will vary somewhat depending on how intensely you reflect the red onto the blue. Reflecting the blue onto the red should produce a similar color.

4. Now for what may be a real surprise, reflect the red light onto the green light. The color you see is yellow. (It may be

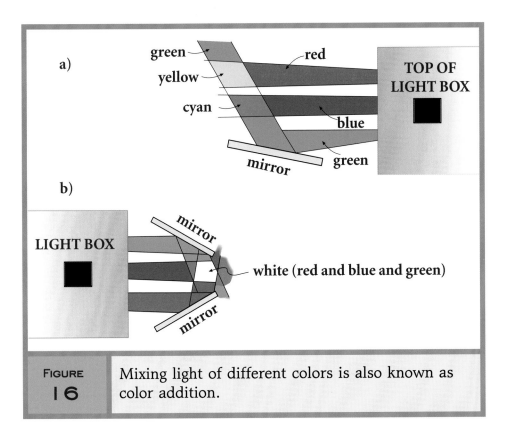

a)

green
yellow
cyan
mirror
red
TOP OF LIGHT BOX
blue
green

b)

LIGHT BOX
mirror
white (red and blue and green)
mirror

| FIGURE 16 | Mixing light of different colors is also known as color addition. |

more orange than yellow if the red is more intense than the green. But you can produce yellow if you make the intensities equal.) Reflecting the green onto the red should produce a similar yellow color.

Red, blue, and green are called the primary colors of light because they can be combined to produce all the other colors you can see. You saw in Experiment 3-1 that white light can be separated into all the colors from violet to red. You might think, therefore, that white light can be produced by combining the primary colors of light. In fact, you can do that by using two mirrors to mix all three colors. You may have to vary the intensities of the different colors, but it can be done as shown in Figure 16b.

A SHADOW WITH COLORED STRIPES

1. **Cover the opening** in the light box with the three-color mask. Lay a piece of white paper in front of the mask. Darken the room and turn on the lightbulb in the light box Use a small piece of clay to support a thin stick or pencil upright in the blue beam close to the light box. Notice the dark shadow cast by the stick.

2. Using a mirror, can you give the shadow a red stripe? Can you give it a green stripe?

3. Using two mirrors, can you give it both a red and a green stripe? How can you give it three stripes—red, green, and yellow?

4. Now support the stick upright in the green beam. Using a mirror, give the shadow a red stripe. Then give it a blue stripe. Using two mirrors, give it both a red and a blue stripe. How can you give it a red, a blue, and a magenta stripe?

 You Will Need

- **light box**
- **three-color mask**
- **white paper**
- **dark room**
- **clay**
- **thin stick or pencil**
- **3 mirrors**
- **a partner**

5. Support the stick upright in the red beam. Using a mirror, give the shadow a blue stripe. Then give it a green stripe. Using two mirrors, give it both a blue and a green stripe. How can you give it a green, a blue, and a cyan stripe?

6. Using three mirrors and a partner to help you, see if you can make part of the shadow white. In other words, make part of the shadow disappear.

IDEA FOR YOUR SCIENCE FAIR

• Where else have you seen colored shadows? Try to explain how each one gets its color.

THE COLOR TRIANGLE

The color triangle (Figure 17) summarizes the mixing of colored lights. The primary colors of light—red, green, and blue—are at the corners of the triangles where two sides come together. Between and connecting the primary colors are the colors you get when you mix two primaries. For example, yellow connects green and red, magenta connects red and blue, and cyan connects blue and green. The white triangle at the center is the color you get when the three primaries mix.

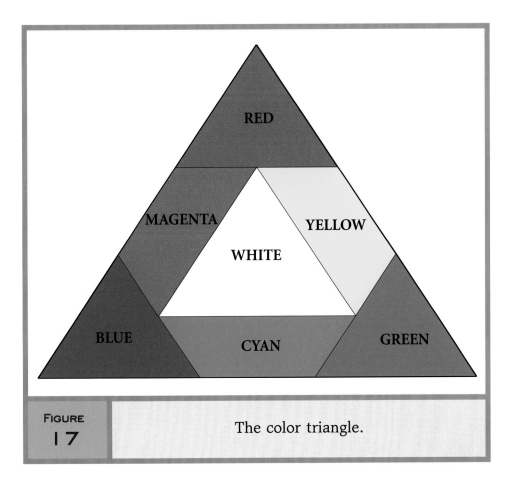

| FIGURE 17 | The color triangle. |

The color on the side opposite a primary is called its complementary color. Yellow is the complementary color of blue; magenta is the complementary color of green; and cyan is the complementary color of red. The combination (mixing) of a primary color and its complementary color should produce white light. Can you explain why?

MIXING A PRIMARY COLOR WITH ITS COMPLEMENTARY COLOR

1. **Cover the opening** in your light box with the three-color mask. Lay a sheet of white paper in front of the mask. Move the mask slightly to one side to leave an opening about 2 cm wide that a narrow beam of white light can pass through. Cover that opening with a strip of yellow filter.

2. Darken the room and turn on the lightbulb in the light box. Use a mirror to reflect blue light, the complementary color of yellow light, onto the yellow beam seen on the white paper. Or reflect the yellow light onto the blue beam. By changing the intensity of the lights as you mix them, can you obtain white light?

You Will Need

- **light box**
- **three-color mask**
- **sheet of white paper**
- **strips of yellow, cyan, and magenta plastic filters**
- **dark room**
- **mirror**

3. Repeat the experiment, but this time cover the opening with a strip of cyan filter. Can you obtain white light by mixing cyan light with red light?

4. Repeat the experiment once more, but this time

cover the opening with two strips of magenta filter. You may find that letting light pass through two magenta filters, one in front of the other, will produce a color that is more truly magenta. Can you obtain white light by mixing magenta light with green light?

SUBTRACTING COLOR FROM LIGHT

It is possible to subtract colors as well as add them. That is what a filter does. Ideally, a red filter allows only red light to pass through it. All the other colors are subtracted (absorbed). Similarly, green filters allow only green light to pass, and blue filters transmit only blue light.

What colors do you think will come through a yellow filter? A cyan filter? A magenta filter?

Paint pigments also subtract color from light. Ideally, an object that is painted red reflects red light and absorbs all the other colors in white light. Similarly, an ideal blue object reflects blue light and absorbs all other colors; a green object absorbs all colors except green, which it reflects.

What colors do you think a yellow object reflects? What colors do you think it will absorb? How about an object with a cyan color? How about a magenta object?

COLORED OBJECTS IN COLORED LIGHT

What do you think a green object looks like in red light? How about a red object in green light? In this experiment you will see how colored objects appear in lights of different colors.

1. Using scissors, cut squares about 10 cm (4 in) on a side from colored construction paper. You will need white, red, yellow, green, blue, and black squares. If possible, include cyan and magenta squares as well.

2. Cover the opening in the light box with the red mask. Lay a sheet of white paper in front of the opening. Turn out all lights except for the bulb in the light box. The room should be completely dark except for the light coming from the light box, which will bathe the white paper with red light.

You Will Need

- **scissors**

- **red, green, and blue masks**

- **colored construction paper—white, red, yellow, green, blue, and black as well as cyan and magenta, if possible**

- **light box**

- **sheet of white paper**

- **very dark room**

3. Place a colored square, each color in turn, so that it lies flat on the white paper in front of the light box. What color do you expect to see if you place a white square in the red light? Try it. Was your prediction correct?

4. Repeat the process for each of the other colored squares. Try to predict what each colored square will look like in red light.

   Which colored squares appeared to be black (or nearly black) in the red light? Can you explain why?

5. Cover the opening in the light box with the green filter. Again, place colored squares, each color in turn, so that they lie flat on the white paper in front of the light box. Try to predict what each colored square will look like in green light. Did the color of any of the squares surprise you? If so, why were you surprised?

6. Finally, cover the opening in the light box with the blue filter. Again, place a colored square, each color in turn, so that it lies flat on the white paper in front of the light box. Try to predict what each colored square will look like in blue light. Did the color of any of the squares surprise you? If so, why were you surprised?

COLORS IN COLORED LIGHT

You may have noticed how the colors of cars and other objects seem to change under yellow sodium vapor lights commonly found in parking lots. Colored objects are colored because they contain colored pigments. These pigments reflect light to your eyes. However, many objects contain more than one pigment and will, therefore, reflect more than one color. You may have found that the blue square appeared green in green light or that the green square appeared blue when bathed by blue light. If they did, they contained more than one colored pigment.

There is another reason why your predictions may not have always been correct. Light filters, like the red, blue, and green ones you used, may not be perfect filters. For example, the blue filter may allow some green or red light to pass through it. The red and green filters may not be perfect either.

In the next experiment, you will find a way to determine what colors come through these filters. With that information, you will be better able to understand why some of your predictions were not correct.

ANALYZING COLOR WITH A DIFFRACTION GRATING

When light passes through a narrow slit, it is diffracted; that is, it spreads out. Different colors are diffracted by different amounts. As a result, colors can be separated by letting light pass through narrow slits.

1. To see how light is diffracted by a narrow slit, turn your light box on its side. Turn the bulb so that the filament is vertical as you view it. Stand about a meter or yard from the light.

Hold two very straight Popsicle sticks so they are side by side and vertical. Separate them by just a tiny bit. You will see the light coming from the bulb's filament spread out after coming through the narrow slit. If you make the slit very narrow, you will see bands of color on both sides of the central beam.

2. Another way to diffract light is to look at the bulb's

You Will Need

- **light box**
- **2 Popsicle sticks**
- **meterstick or yardstick**
- **comb**
- **diffraction grating (borrow from school science department or buy at a hobby shop or from a science supply company)**
- **three-color mask**
- **squares (about 5 cm [2 in]) of yellow, magenta, and cyan filters**

bright filament through a comb. Turn the comb slowly to make the visible space between the comb's teeth smaller. You will see the light spread out and bands of color appear.

A diffraction grating has 5,000 or more slits per centimeter (12,700 or more per inch). With so many narrow slits, the light spreads out into bright spectra (rainbows of color) that can be seen on either side of the bright filament. You may be able to see several spectra by looking to either side of the filament seen through the grating.

3. Pick up the three-color mask. Hold the diffraction grating behind each color (red, blue, and green) in turn. What colors come through the red filter? What colors come through the blue filter? What colors come through the green filter?

Does the red filter let any color other than red pass through it? How about the blue filter? Does it let any color other than blue pass through it? Does the green filter let any color other than green pass through?

4. You have analyzed the colors coming through these filters by using the diffraction grating. Did your analysis help you to understand why some of your predictions in the previous

experiment may have been incorrect? If so, how did it help you?

5. Now try the complementary colors—yellow, cyan, and magenta. Cut squares about 5 cm (2 in) on a side from pieces of yellow, cyan, and magenta filters. (Stack two for magenta.) What colors do you predict will come through each of these colored filters? To find out, hold the yellow filter in front of the diffraction grating and look at the white light coming from the bulb in your light box. What colors come through the filter? Are they the ones you predicted? What colors do not come through the yellow filter?

6. What colors come through the cyan filter? Are they the ones you predicted? What colors do not come through?

7. What colors come through the magenta filter? Are they the ones you predicted? What colors do not come through?

8. What happens if you make filter "sandwiches," two or more filters held together in front of a diffraction grating? Can you predict the colors that will come through a red and a green filter sandwich? How about red and magenta? The chart in Table 1 shows a variety of filter sandwiches. Copy it into your notebook. See if you can fill in the third column in your

TABLE I	Filter color combinations ("sandwiches") chart		
Color of one filter	**Color of other filter(s)**	**Prediction**	**Actual colors seen**
Red	Green		
Red	Blue		
Red	Yellow		
Red	Magenta		
Red	Cyan		
Blue	Green		
Blue	Yellow		
Blue	Magenta		
Blue	Cyan		
Green	Yellow		
Green	Magenta		
Green	Cyan		
Cyan	Magenta		
Cyan	Yellow		
Yellow	Magenta		
Magenta	Yellow+Blue		

notebook by predicting the colors of light that will come through each sandwich. You might predict black if you think no light will come through. Finally, record in your notebook the colors you actually do see.

IDEAS FOR YOUR SCIENCE FAIR

- Look at colored lightbulbs and other lights such as sodium vapor lamps through your diffraction grating. Can you predict what you will see in each case?

- Look at a fluorescent bulb through your diffraction grating. Explain what you see.

MORE ABOUT LIGHT AND COLOR

In Chapter 4 you saw how light of different colors could be added (mixed) to obtain new colors. You saw, too, that colors can be subtracted by passing white light through colored filters. In this chapter, you will subtract color by passing light through colored liquids. You will also explain the colors we often see in the sky, read about a theory of color vision, examine the images you see after looking at bright lights, and observe some mysterious colored shadows.

SUBTRACTING COLORED LIGHT WITH LIQUIDS

You have seen that colored filters can subtract colors from white light. Can colored liquids do the same thing?

1. Nearly fill a clear plastic vial or other small, clear vessel with water. Add a drop or two of green food coloring so that the liquid has a distinct green color.

2. Cover most of the opening in your light box with the wide-slit mask. It will leave an opening about 2 cm (1 in) wide. Be sure the bulb's filament is in a vertical position before you turn on the light.

3. Darken the room and turn on the lightbulb in the light box. Place the green liquid in front of the opening in the light box. Place your diffraction grating between the vial of liquid and your eye. Examine the light that comes through the liquid. The diffraction grating will

 You Will Need

- **clear plastic vial or other small clear vessel**
- **water**
- **green, blue, yellow, and red food coloring**
- **light box**
- **black construction paper**
- **dark room**
- **diffraction grating**
- **a partner**
- **notebook**
- **pen or pencil**

spread the colors that come through the liquid so you can see which colors are absorbed and which colors come through.

If you have difficulty seeing the spectrum, ask someone to help you. Have that person remove and then replace the vial of liquid while you look at the bulb's filament through the diffraction grating.

4. Record the portions of the spectrum that come through the liquid in your notebook. You might find it helpful to make a diagram of the spectrum, such as the one in Figure 18. Which colors does the liquid absorb?

5. Repeat the experiment using blue food coloring. Which colors come through the blue liquid? Which colors are absorbed?

6. What colors are absorbed if you add red food coloring to water in the clear vial? Which colors pass through the liquid?

7. How about yellow food coloring and water? What parts of the spectrum does yellow absorb? What parts does it transmit?

8. Suppose you prepare a liquid that contains two or more food colorings. Based on what you know about the colors each

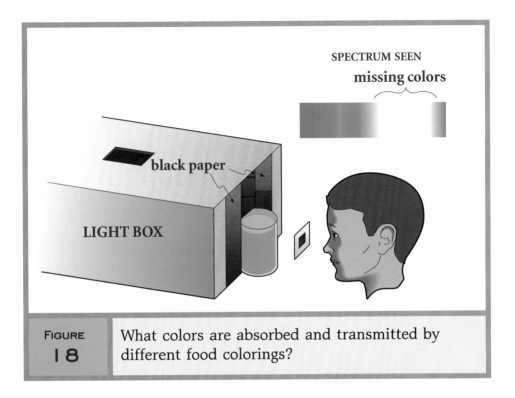

SPECTRUM SEEN

missing colors

black paper

LIGHT BOX

| FIGURE 18 | What colors are absorbed and transmitted by different food colorings? |

absorbs and transmits, can you predict what colors will be absorbed by the mixture? Can you predict what the spectrum will look like when you examine the light that comes through the mixture with a diffraction grating?

9. The chart in Table 2 lists the mixtures you might try. Copy the chart into your notebook. Then see if you can predict the colors that will be absorbed. Draw the spectrum you think you will see through your diffraction grating.

How well did you do? Can you now explain any that you

didn't predict correctly? Do you see what led you to an incorrect prediction?

IDEA FOR YOUR SCIENCE FAIR

What colors are absorbed and transmitted by liquids you drink, such as cranberry juice, lemonade, Gatorade, and others?

TABLE 2	Possible mixtures of water and food coloring for Experiments 5-1		
Mixture of water and food colorings	Colors you predict will be absorbed	Drawing of spectrum you expect to see
Green + blue		
Green + red		
Green + yellow		
Blue + red		
Blue + yellow		
Red + yellow		
Blue + green + yellow		
Blue + green + red		
Blue + green + yellow + red		

When sunlight passes through Earth's atmosphere, some of the light is scattered. This means that molecules of air as well as dust and smoke particles absorb some of the light. Then they release it, but they release the light in all directions—not just in the direction it was traveling when it was absorbed. That is why it is called scattered light.

Scattering is not the same for all colors of light. Blue light is scattered much more than red light. In fact, scattering decreases as you move along the spectrum from violet to blue to green to yellow to orange to red. So red light is scattered very little, while blue light is scattered a lot.

It is the scattering of light that makes the sky blue. The air scatters the blue light in all directions, creating a blue sky on clear days.

1. You can make a model to see how this happens. Leave the opening in the light box uncovered. Place a glass of water near the opening so light from the clear bulb

You Will Need

- **light box**
- **glass of water**
- **spoon**
- **dropper**
- **milk**

passes through the water. The water can represent Earth's atmosphere. The bulb can represent the sun. Add several drops of milk to the water and stir with a spoon. The milk represents particles of air, dust, and smoke.

2. Look at the water from the side. You will see it has acquired a bluish tint. What do you think is producing the bluish color?

    As the sun approaches sunset, its light passes through a greater length of atmosphere. As a result, more blue light is scattered and increasing amounts of green and then yellow light are also scattered. The result is sun that looks red as it reaches the horizon.

3. To see how a sunset is created, look at the clear bulb's filament through the milky water. The bright filament can represent the sun. The filament probably has a slightly yellowish tint because of the blue light that has been scattered in all directions—the blue light you saw from the side of the glass.

4. Add several more drops of milk to the water. Again, look at the bulb through the water. How has its color changed? Why has its color changed? Continue to add drops of milk in small quantities. Look at the bulb each time after you add

drops of milk. How does the color of the bulb change? Can you make a red sunset?

IDEAS FOR YOUR SCIENCE FAIR

- Make a large model of scattering and sunset. Fill a large rectangular fish tank or aquarium with water. Use a slide projector to send a beam of light through the water. Use milk to represent particles in the atmosphere. View the tank from the side to see the scattered blue light. Look at the light through the far end of the tank to see the sun as it approaches sunset.

- Make a diagram and a model to show why sunlight passes through more atmosphere as the sun moves from midday to sunset.

- How can you account for the red sky that is often seen at sunrise?

- Is there any truth to the saying, "Red sky at night, sailors' delight; Red sky at morning, sailors take warning!"?

A THEORY OF COLOR VISION

A theory to explain why we see color was first developed by Thomas Young (1773–1829), an English physicist. His theory was modified and expanded by the German physiologist Hermann von Helmholtz (1821–1894). According to the Helmholtz-Young theory, the central region of the retina has three types of cone cells that respond to color. There are cone cells that respond to red light, cone cells that respond to green light, and cone cells that respond to blue light.

When green light enters our eyes, the cone cells sensitive to green light are stimulated to send signals to our brain and we see green. If red light strikes our retinas, the cone cells sensitive to red light are stimulated to send signals to our brain and we see red. Blue light reaching our retinas causes the cone cells sensitive to blue light to respond and we perceive the color blue.

If yellow light reaches the retina, both red and green cells are stimulated and we see yellow. If both red and green light reach our eyes, we also see yellow, just as you did in Experiment 4-1.

If magenta light falls on our retinas, both the cone cells sensitive to red light and those sensitive to blue light are stimulated and we see a magenta color. If green and blue light enters our eyes, we see the combination as cyan.

The Helmholtz-Young theory of color vision was modified late in the twentieth century by Edwin Land (1909–1991), an American inventor who developed a somewhat more complicated explanation of color vision.

AFTERIMAGES

1. **Look at the bright filament** of the bulb in your light box for several seconds. Then look at a white screen or wall. You continue to see a bright line of light. The light you see is called an afterimage. The retina of your eye continues to be stimulated even after the light has been removed.

2. Leave the opening in your light box uncovered. Lay a sheet of white paper in front of the opening and turn on the light. Place a small green square of construction paper on the white paper directly in front of the opening in the light box. Stare at the green square for about 20 seconds. Then shift your gaze to the white sheet next to the square. You will see an afterimage caused by the green square. Why does the afterimage have a magenta color?

3. Repeat the experiment with a blue square. Why is the afterimage yellow?

You Will Need

- **light box**

- **white cardboard screen or wall**

- **sheet of white paper**

- **colored squares about 10 cm (4 in) on a side made from construction paper—green, blue, red, yellow, cyan, magenta, white, and black**

- **stopwatch or watch with second hand**

4. Repeat the experiment with a red square. Why is the after-image cyan in color?

5. Try to predict the color of the afterimage you will see when you stare at a yellow square. Did you predict correctly?

6. Try to predict the color of the afterimage from a cyan square. Did you predict correctly?

7. Try to predict the color of the afterimage from a magenta square. Did you predict correctly?

8. Suppose you stare at a black square. What do you predict the color of the afterimage will be? Try it! Did you make the correct prediction?

9. How about a white square? Predict the color of the after-image. Try it! Did you make the correct prediction?

The Hemholtz-Young theory of color vision provides an explanation of afterimages. Suppose you stare at a red object. The red cone cells are stimulated. After a time, they become fatigued (tired), just as muscle cells tire with use. If you then look at a white wall, all the colors in white light fall on your retina; however, the "tired" red cone cells do not respond as well as the blue- and green-sensitive cone cells. As a result, you see the complementary color, cyan, on the white wall.

After a time, the red-sensitive cone cells recover and the entire wall again appears white.

According to the theory, what color afterimage would you expect to see after staring at a green square? A blue square? A yellow square? A magenta square? A cyan square?

What colors did you actually see after staring at each of these colored squares?

1. **Set up a white cardboard screen** about 20 cm (8 in) in front of the opening in the light box. Stand a pencil or stick upright about 5 cm (2 in) in front of the screen. Use clay to support the screen and pencil.

2. Cover the light box's entire opening with the green mask. Be sure the bulb's filament is in a vertical position. Darken the room and turn on the lightbulb. You will see the pencil or stick's black shadow on the screen. Nothing mysterious about that!

3. Now move the green mask so it covers only half of the opening in the light box. White light will come out the other side of the opening. Use a mirror to reflect some of the white light onto the pencil or stick so it casts a second shadow on the screen as shown in Figure 19.

4. What is the color of the

 You Will Need

- **white cardboard screen**
- **ruler**
- **light box**
- **pencil or stick**
- **clay**
- **green, blue, and red masks**
- **dark room**
- **mirror**

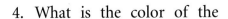

shadow cast by the white light you reflected? Can you explain its color? Now look at the mysterious color of the original shadow, which is still in green light. You can probably see that it is magenta, the complementary color of green. Why does it have a magenta color?

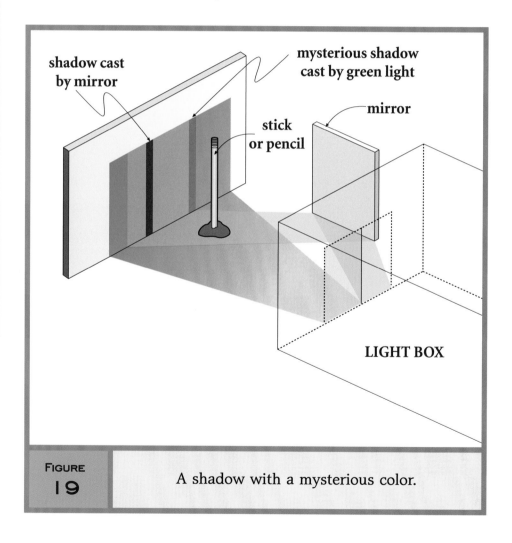

shadow cast by mirror

mysterious shadow cast by green light

mirror

stick or pencil

LIGHT BOX

FIGURE 19

A shadow with a mysterious color.

5. Repeat the experiment, using the blue mask instead of the green mask. What colors do you expect the shadows to have? Were you right? Can you explain the shadows' colors?

6. Repeat the experiment once more using the red mask. What colors do you expect the shadows to have? Were you right? Can you explain the shadows' colors? Does what you know about afterimages and the theory of color vision help you to explain the mysterious shadows?

*Arbor Scientific
P.O. Box 2750
Ann Arbor, MI 48106-2750
(800) 367-6695
http://www.arborsci.com

Carolina Biological Supply Co.
2700 York Road
Burlington, NC 27215-3398
(800) 334-5551
http://www.carolina.com

Connecticut Valley Biological
Supply Co., Inc.
82 Valley Road, Box 326
Southampton, MA 01073
(800) 628-7748
http://www.ctvalleybio.com/

Delta Education
P.O. Box 3000
80 Northwest Blvd.
Nashua, NH 03061-3000
(800) 258-1302
http://www.delta-education.com

**Edmund Scientific
60 Pearce Avenue
Tonawanda, NY 14150-6711
(800) 728-6999
http://www.scientificsonline.com

Educational Innovations, Inc.
362 Main Avenue
Norwalk, CT 06851
(888) 912-7474
http://www.teachersource.com

Fisher Science Education
4500 Turnberry Drive
Hanover Park, IL 60133
(800) 955-1177
http://www.fishersci.com

Frey Scientific
P.O. Box 8101
100 Paragon Parkway
Mansfield, OH 44903
(800) 225-3739
http://www.freyscientific.com

Nasco-Fort Atkinson
P.O. Box 901
901 Janesville Avenue
Fort Atkinson, WI 53538-0901
(800) 558-9595
http://www.nascofa.com/

Nasco-Modesto
P.O. Box 3837
4825 Stoddard Road
Modesto, CA 95352-3837
(800) 558-9595
http://www.enasco.com

***Products on Demand
265 Dundee Road
Stanford, CT 06903
203-322-1774
http://www.productsondemand.biz

Sargent-Welch/VWR Scientific
P.O. Box 4130
Buffalo, NY 14217
(800) 727-4368
http://www.SargentWelch.com

Science Kit & Boreal Laboratories
777 East Park Drive
P.O. Box 5003
Tonawanda, NY 14150
(800) 828-7777
http://www.sciencekit.com

Wards Natural Science
P.O. Box 92912
5100 West Henrietta Road
Rochester, NY 14692-9012
(800) 962-2660
http://www.wardsci.com/

*Arbor Scientific has a kit of six 8 x 10-inch color filters.

**Edmund Scientific has large sheets of red, blue, and green filters. The catalog numbers are A30351-35 (blue), A30351-36 (green), and A30351-37 (red). They do not have yellow, cyan, or magenta filters, which you also need to perform several of the color experiments.

***Products on Demand sells Roscolene color filters (gels) at reasonable prices. Their Gold Star Basic kit contains ten 6½ in x 6½ in filters with all the colors and material you need for experiments. The table below lists the colored filters

Color According to This Book	Color According to Roscolene	Products on Demand Order Number
red	orange	R-818
red (option)	orange + follies pink	R-818 + R-828
green	light green	R-871
blue	surprise blue	R-861
yellow	straw	R-809
cyan	green blue	R-859
cyan (option)	medium blue green	R-877
magenta	follies pink	R-828

needed for the experiments in this book, the Roscolene color name, and the Products on Demand order number.

You may order color gels on two other Web sites: **http://www.stagelightingstore.com** and **http://www.djdepot.com/zprogelsh-gel-sheet-p-345.html.**

FURTHER READING

Bardhan-Quallen, Sudipta. *Championship Science Fair Projects: 100 Sure-To-Win Experiments.* New York: Sterling Publishing, 2004.

Bochinski, Julianne Blair. *More Award-Winning Science Fair Projects.* Hoboken, N.J.: John Wiley and Sons, 2004.

DiSpezio, Michael A. *Super Sensational Science Fair Projects.* New York: Sterling Publishing, 2002.

Gardner, Robert. *Light, Sound, and Waves Science Fair Projects Using Sunglasses, Guitars, CDs, and Other Stuff.* Berkeley Heights, N.J.: Enslow Publishers, 2004.

Hamilton, Gina L. *Light: Prisms, Rainbows, and Colors.* Chicago: Raintree, 2004.

Jackson, Tom. *Light and Color.* Danbury, Conn.: Grolier Educational, 2002.

Krieger, Melanie Jacobs. *How to Excel in Science Competitions: Revised and Updated.* Berkeley Heights, N.J.: Enslow Publishers, 1999.

Rhatigan, Joe, and Rain Newcomb. *Prize-Winning Science Fair Projects for Curious Kids.* New York: Lark Books, 2004.

Tocci, Salvatore. *Experiments with Light.* New York: Children's Press, 2001.

Walker, Sally M. *Light.* Minneapolis: Lerner Publications, 2006.

Bob Miller's Light Walk.
   http://www.exploratorium.edu/light_walk

Optics for Kids.
   http://www.opticalres.com/kidoptx_f.html

INDEX

ABOUT THE AUTHOR

Robert Gardner is an award-winning author of science books for young people. A retired high school teacher of physics, chemistry, and physical science, he enjoys writing, biking, and doing volunteer work.

For my three favorite bears—
Peter, Laura, and Bill!
—A. S. C.

For Eunice and Sally
with love and thanks
—L. H.

Henry Holt and Company
Publishers since 1866
175 Fifth Avenue, New York, New York 10010
mackids.com

Henry Holt® is a registered trademark of Macmillan Publishing Group, LLC.
Text copyright © 2017 by Alyssa Satin Capucilli
Illustrations copyright © 2017 by Lorna Hussey
All rights reserved.

Library of Congress Cataloging-in-Publication Data is available.
ISBN 978-1-62779-701-6

Our books may be purchased in bulk for promotional, educational, or business use.
Please contact your local bookseller or the Macmillan Corporate and Premium Sales Department at
(800) 221-7945 ext. 5442 or by e-mail at MacmillanSpecialMarkets@macmillan.com.

First Edition—2017
The illustrations for this book were created with watercolor and graphite.
Printed in China by RR Donnelley Asia Printing Solutions Ltd.,
Dongguan City, Guangdong Province

1 3 5 7 9 10 8 6 4 2

THIS BEAR'S BIRTHDAY

Alyssa Satin Capucilli

Illustrated by Lorna Hussey

Henry Holt and Company
New York

It was Bear's birthday. Papa measured Bear
by the tall oak tree.

"You're getting bigger every day, Bear. You
can do lots of things all by yourself now."

Bear smiled. He liked to do things with
Mama and Papa. He liked to do things all by
himself, too.

"It's time to get dressed for your birthday party," said Mama.

"This bear can get dressed all by himself," said Bear.

Bear put on his shirt

and pants

and shiny green boots.

But no matter how he tried, Bear couldn't put on his jacket.

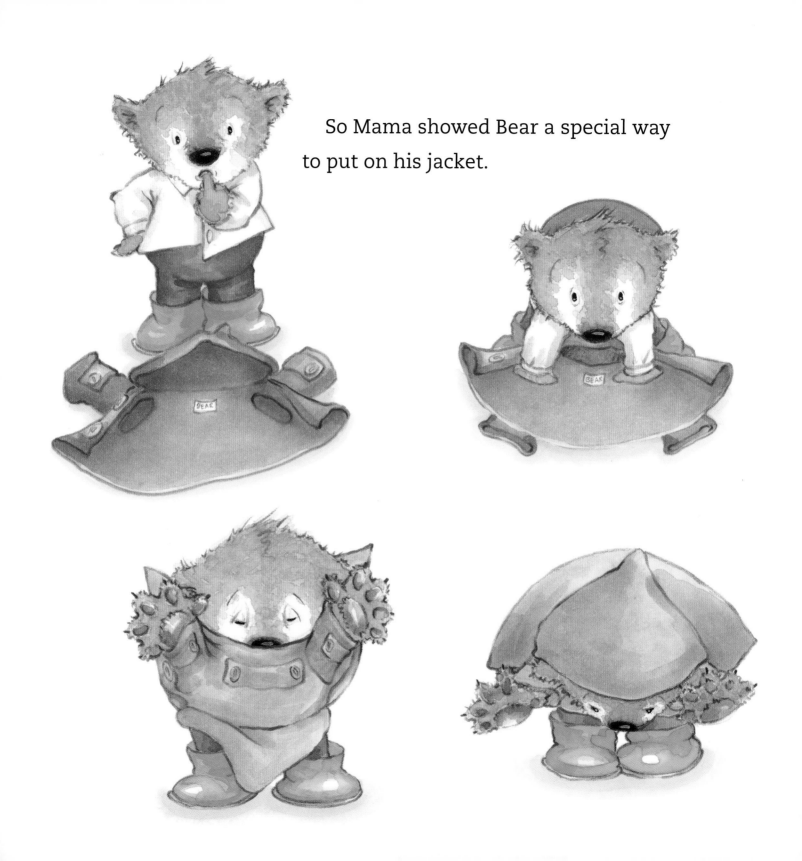

So Mama showed Bear a special way
to put on his jacket.

"This bear *can* get
dressed all by himself,"
said Bear.

"Let's pick some apples for
your birthday cake," said Papa.

"This bear can pick apples all by himself," said Bear.

Bear stretched up high. He jumped and jumped—but the apples were just out of reach!

Papa put Bear on his shoulders.
"Try again, Bear."
Bear reached out and picked
the shiniest apples he could find.
"This bear *can* pick apples all
by himself," said Bear.

"Who can help make peanut butter and honey sandwiches for the party?" asked Mama. "This bear can!" said Bear.

Bear tugged and tugged,
but the peanut butter jar was
hard to open.

"Try now, Bear," said Mama
as she helped loosen the lid.

Bear spread the peanut butter
and drizzled the honey. It was
sticky, but it was sweet, too!

There really were lots of
things he could do all by
himself.

When Bear's friends arrived, it was time to play hide-and-seek. Then there was a puppet show, songs to sing, and a delicious picnic lunch.

Suddenly, a gust of wind blew!
Red, yellow, and orange leaves
came tumbling down.

"This bear can put
the leaves back on the
tree all by himself,"
called Bear.

Bear tossed the leaves high and he threw the leaves wide, but the leaves kept falling back to the ground.

"I may be getting bigger," said Bear, "but this bear can't put the leaves back on the tree."

"Oh, Bear," said Papa, "there are some things that no bear can do."

"No matter how big you are," said Mama.

Bear looked at the colorful leaves. "Maybe there is something all of us bears can do . . . ," said Bear.

So the bears raked and raked. And when the pile was bigger than even the very biggest bear, they all jumped in together!

Soon it was time for birthday cake.
Bear closed his eyes and made a wish,
and then he blew out every candle.

"This bear did it," said Bear with a
smile, "all by himself!"

"Happy birthday, Bear!" said
Mama and Papa. And they gave Bear
the very first slice.